T0353924

SERIES 228

In this book, we travel back in time to
ancient Egypt to learn about pyramids,
mummies, gods and goddesses, pharaohs,
hieroglyphs and much, much more.

LADYBIRD BOOKS
UK | USA | Canada | Ireland | Australia
India | New Zealand | South Africa
Ladybird Books is part of the Penguin Random House group of companies
whose addresses can be found at global.penguinrandomhouse.com.
www.penguin.co.uk   www.puffin.co.uk   www.ladybird.co.uk

Penguin
Random House
UK

First published 2022
001
Copyright © Ladybird Books Ltd, 2022
Printed in China

The authorized representative in the EEA is Penguin Random House Ireland,
Morrison Chambers, 32 Nassau Street, Dublin D02 YH68

A CIP catalogue record for this book is available from the British Library
ISBN: 978-0-241-54417-4
All correspondence to:
Ladybird Books
Penguin Random House Children's
One Embassy Gardens, 8 Viaduct Gardens
London SW11 7BW

The Ancient Egyptians

A Ladybird Book

Written by Sidra Ansari
with Egyptologist, Dr Marina Escolano-Poveda

Illustrated by Anja Sušanj

Ancient Egypt

The ancient Egyptian civilization began around 3100 BCE, when the people who lived alongside the River Nile, in Northeast Africa, became organized as one unified kingdom. The civilization lasted for over 3,000 years, and Egyptologists – people who study ancient Egypt – divide the history into five significant time spans:

- The Old Kingdom: 2700 to 2200 BCE

- The Middle Kingdom: 2050 to 1650 BCE

- The New Kingdom: 1550 to 1100 BCE

- The Late Period: 1100 to 343 BCE

- The Graeco-Roman Period: 332 BCE to 395 CE

During these time frames, the country was usually ruled by kings or queens called "pharaohs". Between these time spans, there were "intermediate periods" – times of unrest often marked by famine, plagues or war.

The ancient Egyptians developed new ideas and inventions that have shaped the world as we know it today. They invented mathematics, geometry, astronomy, writing, paper, medicine, the ramp, the lever and the plough, to name just a few! Many remarkable landmarks from this ancient civilization are still standing today. People from all over the world travel to Egypt to see the amazing temples and pyramids that tell us so much about ancient Egyptian life.

Life on the river

The Nile flows for over 4,100 miles (6,600 km) until it reaches the Mediterranean Sea. It is the longest river in the world and runs through several countries, including Egypt, Sudan, Ethiopia, Uganda and Burundi.

Egypt has always been a very hot country mostly made up of desert land, so the river was a hugely important part of life. It flooded every year, soaking the surrounding fields. The ancient Egyptians believed this flooding was a gift from the gods because it left behind moist, dark soil that was perfect for growing crops. The ancient Egyptians called the flood plains *Kemet*, which means "the black one", referring to the colour of the land.

The most important crops that were grown around the Nile were wheat, barley, flax and papyrus. Papyrus plants grew along the river and were used to make sandals, ropes, mats, cords and – most valuable of all – paper. Papyrus was also used to make small boats called "skiffs".

The ancient Egyptians used the Nile as an important highway. It carried people and goods up and down its length, bringing riches to and from Egypt. The river was used to transport building materials such as limestone and sandstone, which were used to make the pyramids. The mud on the riverbanks was also used to make sun-dried bricks for houses and other buildings.

Top of the "pyramid"

The hierarchy of society in ancient Egypt was shaped like a pyramid. At the top sat the pharaoh. The ancient Egyptians believed the pharaoh had sacred powers and a divine position given to them by the gods. A pharaoh's job was to keep the gods happy, manage the laws and protect the land. Viziers were very important advisors to the pharaoh. They helped make judgements and were in charge of the government. Priests and priestesses were powerful people who were responsible for looking after the temples.

Soldiers were held in high regard and, if they survived battle, were given rewards. Scribes were much-valued people who could read and write. They kept the government records up to date, and they also wrote beautiful poems and stories. Farmers produced food and crops, so they were a vital part of society. There were also craftsmen who produced goods such as pottery, clothes and metal items such as jewellery.

Sadly, some individuals were enslaved. "Slavery" is the name for the horrible practice of people owning other people. Most information about slavery in ancient Egypt comes from the New Kingdom. Enslaved people mostly came from outside of Egypt and were prisoners of war. They were forced to work in dangerous jobs, such as mining. Tragically, many enslaved people lost their lives doing so. Other enslaved people – especially women – worked as household servants and could sometimes be freed by their enslavers.

Pharaohs

The word "pharaoh" comes from the phrase "great house", which refers to the big palaces where the pharaohs lived. They lived in great luxury and were surrounded by people who attended to their every need. The pharaoh would have many duties to fulfil throughout the day. They would visit temples to make offerings to the gods and goddesses. When a pharaoh left the palace, they would travel through the city in their royal chariot. Many people would leave their daily jobs to rush to attend their ruler's procession.

A pharaoh usually wore a half-pleated kilt around their body and, as symbols of power, a broad collar over their shoulders and a lion's tail hanging from their belt. They also wore a crown or headcloth, and a fake beard. They are often depicted holding a crook and flail – the crook represented kingship, and the flail represented fertility of the land.

Some pharaohs were very young when they came to power. One of the most famous, Tutankhamun, became pharaoh at the age of nine! Although pharaohs all did the same job, they often had very different ambitions and ways of ruling. One of the most ambitious pharaohs was Ramses II. He ordered more statues to be built of himself than any other pharaoh, and also replaced the names of earlier kings on their monuments with his own – so we think he may have been quite arrogant!

Women in power

Of the approximately 170 pharaohs who ruled throughout the history of ancient Egypt, only seven of them were women. While that may sound like a small number, there were actually more female rulers in ancient Egypt than any other ancient civilization. Many women were only given positions of power so they could stand in for men. However, some of the most memorable pharaohs were women, and they made their mark on history.

Queen Hatshepsut ruled on behalf of her nephew, until she decided it was time to officially take charge. She declared herself pharaoh and cleverly had herself depicted in works of art as the daughter of the god Amun-Ra. She wore the same fake beard as male pharaohs.

Queen Nefertiti ruled alongside her husband, Akhenaten, and may have ruled after his death. She is often depicted in positions of authority. Her name meant "the beautiful one has arrived", but Egyptologists think she was far more than this suggests and was a very powerful leader.

Greek queen Cleopatra was the last pharaoh. She gained the love of Julius Caesar, the ruler of the Roman Empire, and Mark Antony, a Roman general, and used her power to wage war against her brother to take over Egypt. She was a very educated woman who could speak many languages and became a patron of the arts and sciences.

Writing history

In ancient Egypt, all writing was done by scribes, who had the important job of keeping records of everything. Only wealthier families could afford to send their children to school to become scribes.

The Egyptian word for scribe is *sesh*, which also means "to write". Egyptian can be written in three scripts. One script is called "hieroglyphs" and is made up of symbols. There are over 700 hieroglyphic symbols, and each one can mean more than one thing. For example, a picture of an owl can mean "owl" or it can indicate the sound "m".

Scribes needed various tools to write, including a wooden palette, ink, reed pens and brushes. Paper was made from papyrus reeds, while pens and brushes were made from reed stems. As paper made from papyrus took a long time to make and was expensive, scribes practised on pieces of broken clay vessels called *ostraca*.

It took Egyptologists a long time to understand what hieroglyphs meant. The discovery of the Rosetta Stone in 1799 helped them to unlock the code. The stone is engraved with hieroglyphs, demotic script and Greek script, so they were able to translate the Greek, and the code was successfully cracked in 1822 by scholar Jean-François Champollion.

Can you write your name using the hieroglyphic symbols on the page opposite?

Mummies and the afterlife

The ancient Egyptians believed that when a person died, they would live on in the afterlife. They thought that if a person was buried with everything important to them from this life, they could carry those things with them into the next.

They used a process called "mummification" to preserve dead bodies so that people could use their bodies again in the afterlife. They even mummified pets so they could take them with them, too. The whole process of mummification took around 70 days to complete.

They began by drying and embalming the flesh. First, they used salt to remove any moisture, and then they used resins and oils to preserve the flesh. Then, the liver, lungs, intestines and stomach were removed from the body and preserved in large jars called "canopic jars". The brain was removed by using hooked instruments to pull it out through the nostrils. The heart was left inside the body, as the ancient Egyptians believed it was the centre of the person's being. They would plump out bits of the body using linen, and even put in fake eyes to make the body look more lifelike.

Next, they would wrap the whole body with metres and metres of linen. Before the body was laid to rest, a priest performed a ritual that involved touching its mouth. They believed this would allow the person to be able to breathe, speak and eat in the afterlife.

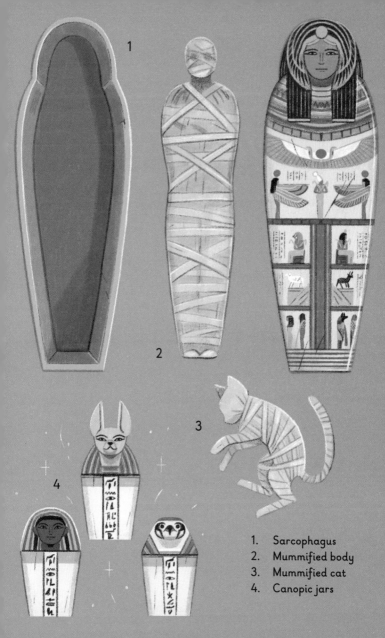

1. Sarcophagus
2. Mummified body
3. Mummified cat
4. Canopic jars

Building the pyramids

Pyramids are gigantic tombs that were mostly built for pharaohs. When a pharaoh died, their mummified body was buried in a pyramid alongside their personal belongings. For years, archaeologists thought that the special texts, secret passageways and false doors that they discovered in the pyramids were there to deter tomb raiders. However, they now believe that they were actually placed there as important signposts to guide the dead on their journey to the afterlife.

One of the largest pyramids is called the Great Pyramid of Giza, also known as the "Horizon of Khufu". It was one of the Seven Wonders of the Ancient World, and it still stands today. Over time, wind, sand and stone robbers have changed its size, but it once stood at a height of around 150 metres (500 ft). It was the tallest structure in the world for almost 4,000 years! The pyramid was made from 2.3 million blocks of rock and would have taken at least 20,000 workers over 23 years to build.

Pyramids were built before the invention of pulleys and wheels, so it would have been an incredible amount of work. Workers would have transported limestone from quarries by boat along the Nile. They also used wooden sledges to transport the heavy rock. Egyptologists think they would have cut up the large blocks, then slowly moved them up the pyramid on ramps to build it up one block at a time.

Gods and goddesses

The ancient Egyptians believed in thousands of gods and goddesses. They believed these gods controlled the universe, so it was important to keep them happy! The ancient Egyptians had different stories explaining the creation of the universe. In the story followed in the city of Memphis, the god Ptah created the universe through his thoughts and words.

Gods and goddesses were often depicted as animals, or as humans with animal heads. Anubis, the jackal-headed god, was the god of embalming and looked after the dead. Many gods represented elements, like Shu, the god of air, who holds the goddess of the sky, Nut, and separates her from Geb, the god of the earth.

Geb and Nut had five children: Osiris, Isis, Seth, Nephthys and Horus the Elder. Of all their children, Osiris was favoured and became king of Egypt. He ruled the land as the first-ever pharaoh, but his brother Seth was jealous and killed him. Isis – the goddess of magic – was the wife of Osiris. She helped bring him back to life. However, Osiris told her that he belonged in the afterlife, and from then on he was known as the god of the underworld. Isis had a son named Horus – the god of kingship – who helped restore harmony to the land by defeating his uncle, Seth. Horus injured his eye during this fight, but it magically healed. The eye then became the symbol of powerful healing.

1. Anubis
2. Isis
3. Horus
4. Osiris
5. Ptah

Towering temples

Temples of all shapes and sizes were built across the land of ancient Egypt. Most of these temples were built as houses for gods or goddesses. Only the pharaoh, priests, priestesses and other officials were allowed to go inside these temples. During some festivals, however, ordinary people could access some areas of the temple precincts, such as the courtyards. Inside the temples, priests and priestesses performed various rituals. They re-enacted stories from the lives and origins of the gods and goddesses. They used it as a space to ward off evil, to ask for help through prayer and to give food offerings to the gods and goddesses.

Great temples were constructed on the east and west banks of the Nile. One of the largest was the temple of Karnak, which included many different buildings that together made one huge temple complex. The Great Hypostyle Hall was its largest room, containing 134 huge pillars which were covered in hieroglyphs – some of the pillars stretched as high as 21 metres (70 ft) tall! Abu Simbel was another impressive temple and was built for Ramses II and his wife, Nefertari. It was made up of two massive rock-cut temples, and four huge statues of Ramses II mark the entrance.

Today, most of the temples that still stand are a sandy colour, but thousands of years ago they would have been painted with colourful artwork – a bright and dazzling spectacle to behold.

Festivals

Hieroglyphs and artwork found on tombs and temples show us how important the celebration of seasonal festivals was to the ancient Egyptians. The most important festivals were held at the beginning of the year and the summer flood.

Festivals were displays of spiritual connections, abundance in agriculture and great wealth. The festivals helped people connect with the gods and goddesses and would involve food, re-enactions of religious stories, and trading of goods.

Many festivals were national, and people from all parts of the country celebrated. They were very happy occasions, and the streets would be full of people. Many people brought offerings to the gods and goddesses, which they shared with the priest and the local people to celebrate the event. To ensure liveliness, musicians played in the streets all day.

The Festival of Opet was in celebration of the time of joyous renewal at the city of Thebes. When the riverbanks flooded, the ancient Egyptians would gather together and celebrate in style! Statues of supreme god Amun-Ra and his family were placed in special vessels and carried along in an impressive procession from Karnak to Luxor. It was one of the most famous festivals and was attended by huge crowds each year.

The Great Sphinx

A sphinx is a legendary creature with the body of a lion and the head of a human or another creature. It appears in ancient myths and old stories. The ancient Egyptians carved these creatures out of rock and positioned them to guard areas such as tombs and temples. The statues had the head of a pharaoh or god, and were usually enormous and very impressive. There are many sphinxes in and around Egypt. In the ancient city of Thebes, there were said to be over 900 shown with the head of a ram to represent the god Amun-Ra. These were placed along the paths that led to the temples, in particular connecting the temples of Karnak and Luxor.

The largest sphinx is called the Great Sphinx. It sits outside the pyramids in Giza, guarding their entrances. It is a huge sculpture which is 73 metres (240 ft) long and 20 metres (66 ft) high. Egyptologists believe it was carved from one huge block of limestone in honour of Pharaoh Khafra. It is still standing today but has been worn down by wind, sand and vandalism, and it is missing its nose! Egyptologists believe that the Great Sphinx would have once been painted in bright colours.

The Great Sphinx has become a symbol, appearing on coins, stamps and official documents. Many people are worried about the effect of the environment and pollution on it and are working to protect it from future damage.

Family life

The ancient Egyptians usually lived in family units composed of two parents and, on average, three to five children. Other family members, such as aunts or grandmothers, sometimes shared the house, too. Wealthy families could also have several servants.

Many children in ancient Egypt didn't go to school. From as young as five years old, they would help their parents with work such as fishing or trading at the market. That's why children were considered a great gift and blessing – they could help with chores! Children – usually boys – who had wealthier parents would go to school and learn mathematics, reading and writing. When a girl turned fourteen, her parents would start to look for a husband for her. Boys married when they were older.

It didn't matter what part of society you came from – young or old, rich or poor, all spent a lot of time outdoors. Playing athletic sports and staying fit was a huge part of their lives.

The ancient Egyptians kept many animals as pets, including cats and dogs. The saluki was one of the most popular breeds of dog. Whippets were the royal dogs of the pharaohs – they were likely to be the puppies of greyhounds crossed with pariah dogs. They were small, fast hunting dogs. There were also wild dogs and strays that hunted around the outside of villages – and still do today!

Fashion

Clothing in ancient Egypt was mostly made from linen cloth – the same material that was used to wrap up mummies! The Egyptians made linen from the fibres of the flax plant. They would hire workers – mostly women – to spin the fibres into a thread. This would then be woven into a linen fabric using looms. It was a lengthy and demanding process.

The linen was typically white and rarely dyed another colour. It was often made into long, simple tunics, some of which had long sleeves. Most clothing was wrapped around the body and then held on with a belt. It was the perfect clothing for the hot and dry climate, as it helped them to keep cool. Children often didn't wear clothes until they were around six years old.

Wealthy people wore very soft linen clothes made from thin fibres, and they decorated dresses using beads or feathers. Ordinary people who had less money usually wore rougher linen clothing made from thicker fibres.

Children are often depicted as wearing their hair in sidelocks, which were a symbol of youth. Many wealthy men and women shaved off their hair and instead wore wigs to protect them from the sun. They often soaked these wigs with perfume. They all took great pride in their appearance and hoped to stand out from the crowd.

Glittering gold

Both men and women wore make-up in ancient Egypt, but it wasn't just about appearance. They often wore it to protect their skin from the sun, too.

Common make-up ingredients included a copper ore called "malachite", which was used to make a popular green eye make-up. Malachite powder made the eyes appear larger and protected those who wore it from the sun's strong rays. Kohl was made from minerals, such as galena. It was used to draw thick black lines around the eyes to give them an almond shape. It also shielded the eyes from the sun.

Red ochre was used as a blusher for the cheeks or lip colour, and henna was used to colour the fingertips and toes. They are still widely used as natural dyes by many women worldwide today.

Once they gathered the ingredients for their make-up, ancient Egyptians prepared the mixture so that it was ready to apply. The raw minerals were ground into a powder and then mixed with animal fat to make it easy to apply and stay on the skin.

Men and women also wore elaborate jewellery, from shining rings to brightly coloured pendants. Wearing lots of jewellery was often a sign of great wealth or status. Many people wore amulets, which were small pieces of jewellery that were considered to be magical and to offer protection.

Toys and games

The ancient Egyptians spent a lot of time working, but they also loved to play games, including board games. One of these was called "Hounds and Jackals", and the rules were very similar to the game Snakes and Ladders that you might play today.

Even the pharaohs had a favourite game. It was called "Senet" and was played on a rectangular checked board. There were 30 squares on the board, and each player had to try to get their counters to the end first. Historians believe that some squares may have been unlucky to land on and might have sent players right back to the start. Senet also had associations with the afterlife. *The Book of the Dead*, a text that describes the journey to the afterlife, depicts the dead playing a game of Senet without an opponent, which has been interpreted as a reference to this journey.

People also played tug of war, in which two teams pull on opposite sides of a rope. The team that pulled the hardest won, while the other team fell on the ground! Around 100 years ago, tug of war was so popular that it was even part of the Olympic Games.

Children enjoyed other sports, such as wrestling, racing, leapfrog and dancing. They would also play an ancient version of hockey by hitting a leather ball with a stick made out of palm leaves.

1. Senet
2. Hounds and Jackals

Telling the time

The ancient Egyptians didn't have modern-day clocks.
They used water clocks, known as "clepsydras", to measure
the passing of time. These were vessels made of stone or
clay with a series of markings on the inside and a little hole
at the bottom. They were filled with water, and as the water
poured through the little hole, time could be measured using
the markings. The clocks often had astronomical decoration
on their outer part.

The ancient Egyptians were also one of the first civilizations
to invent calendars. They created a solar calendar based
on the movement of the sun, which they used for most of
their daily affairs. They also had a lunar calendar based
on the moon's cycle, but it was only used for religious
festivals. The solar calendar had twelve months made up
of 30 days each.

Farmers divided their year into three seasons based on the
cycles of the River Nile. First was the flooding season (*Akhet*),
which ran from June to September. Then came the growing
season (*Peret*) from October to February, as the floodwaters
left behind a rich, black soil layer – perfect for growing
crops in abundance. Finally, in March, the harvesting season
began (*Shemu*).

Magical medicine

Medicine in ancient Egypt combined practical procedures – for instance the use of medicinal herbs and the physical treatment of injuries – with a strong belief in magic, the gods, demons and evil spirits.

The ancient Egyptians had a detailed knowledge of anatomy, and had identified the most important organs inside the body, including the lungs, stomach, intestines, liver and heart. However, they thought that the heart was the thinking organ and the place where the personality of each person resided. They thought that the brain was just there to fill the skull. Their theory was that these organs were connected by a series of channels through which fluids like blood, saliva or urine circulated. Spirits could enter the body through these channels, so people needed to be protected with amulets and magical spells.

Ancient Egyptian doctors created scrolls that detailed lots of scientific procedures. These scrolls are now the oldest medical documents in the world. They contain information on all sorts of things, from treating skin problems, dental problems and eye diseases to how to set broken bones and treat burns. Many of the amazing observations and practical solutions that ancient Egyptian doctors and healers made have led the way for modern medicine as we know it today.

Rediscovering ancient Egypt

In the late nineteenth and early twentieth centuries, new discoveries sparked a huge wave of archaeological interest in ancient Egypt from other parts of the world. The most significant of these came on 26 November 1922, when British archaeologist Howard Carter and his team found the tomb of Tutankhamun. The team discovered steps leading to the tomb in the Valley of the Kings. The tomb was, miraculously, completely intact and contained over 5,000 items including games, statues, chariots and Tutankhamun's mummified body. The most iconic treasure to be discovered was the pharaoh's golden burial mask.

Uncovered treasures of ancient Egypt are housed in museums such as the Grand Egyptian Museum in Giza and the National Museum of Egyptian Civilization in Cairo, but many are no longer in Egypt. For example, a 3,500-year-old bust of Queen Nefertiti, which is considered one of the most critical artefacts to come out of ancient Egypt, is now kept in Germany. The famous Rosetta Stone now sits in the British Museum, London.

Many countries have taken Egypt's ancient treasures for themselves, but there are lots of people who believe the treasures should be returned. Next time you visit a museum, have a look at where the artefacts have come from. How do you think they got there? What does it tell you about history?

A Ladybird Book

collectable books for curious kids

The Ancient Egyptians

9780241544174

British Kings and Queens

9780241544167

The Romans

9780241544181

The Stone Age

9780241544198

 SERIES 228

Collect them all!

SERIES 208

- ☐ Animal Habitats
- ☐ Baby Animals
- ☐ Insects and Minibeasts
- ☐ Sea Creatures
- ☐ Trees

SERIES 218

- ☐ Electricity
- ☐ The Human Body
- ☐ The Solar System
- ☐ Trains
- ☐ Weather

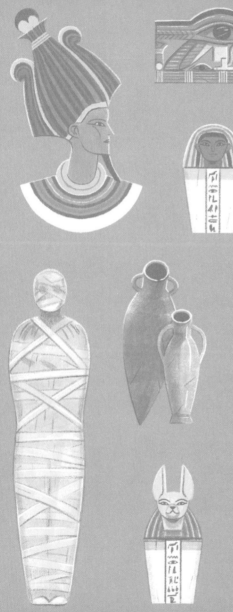